Hobby Horses Will Dance...

This first collection of poetry is based on myth, nature and folklore, sprinkled with a touch of Anglo-Saxon.

Follow the months of the year as those before would have done, and enjoy.

Hobby Horses Will Dance...

Margaret Holbrook

Empress Publishing

Copyright © Margaret Holbrook, 2014

All rights reserved

Published by Empress Publishing, Cheshire.

ISBN 978-0-9929685-1-9

October 2014

The rights of the author have been asserted.

No part of this publication may be reproduced, stored in a retrieval system, or transmitted, in any form or by any means, electronic, mechanical, photocopying, recording or otherwise, without the prior permission of the publisher or copyright owner.

Photograph of Remains of Trentham Hall used with permission of the Trentham Estate.
All photographs, Copyright © Margaret Holbrook 2014

About This Book

When I decided to write poems based on the months of the year, I knew there had to be references to our folklore and traditions, and also our Anglo-Saxon heritage.

These are subjects I am keenly interested in, and it would give me a plenty of scope.

The beauty of folklore is in the telling. We have to keep these traditions alive or they are lost, gone forever. I would be devastated if that were to happen.

So on reading the poems, firstly, I hope that you enjoy them for the poems they are, and secondly, that they may remind you of those stories that your grandma told you, but that you only half-listened to.

Enjoy reading them, (aloud if you want to; they are good in the telling,) and as you work your way through you will find that some of the poems have explanatory notes at the foot of the page. For more detailed notes, see *Author's Notes* at the back of the book.

Margaret Holbrook

Contents

Exits and Entrances (Aefter Yule)   1

The Little Month   3

The Lenten Days   4

April   5

Tri Milchi Monath   6

The Dry Month   7

July   9

Woed Monath   10

Barley Month   12

Wyn Monath   13

Old Ninth   14

Yule Monath   16

As a Child...	18
Anas Platyrhynchos	19
May at Tittesworth	20
May	21
Ladybird	22
The Bumble Bee	23
Lizard Point	25
A View of Autumn	26
To Earth, A Love Poem	27
Echinoderms	28
Haiku. A Winter Theme	29
Notes on Poems	30

viiii

x

Exits and Entrances (Aefter Yule)

Once, he came too soon
and frost and ice was
spread in December.
Too early for the folks
who enjoy warm,
damp, Christmas mornings.
But, when he did arrive
and stand at the doorway
of the year,
it was with a show of
bright-blue skies and sunny,
frost-filled mornings.
Not bleak or deep, not yet.
That came later,
on cue, with the
deft flick of an unseen switch.
Crisp and deep and even
for days and nights and weeks.
Epiphany came and went.
Twelfth night cake was eaten.
And on the ninth, a sacrificial
ram for Janus?
No!
The winter continued.
As for Hilary,
coldness spread, the thirteenth
found frost on twig and earth.

Those who remained,
un-seen, could remember
a past when ale and wine
were as ice.
And on the eve of St Agnes,
we may see that maiden?
The one to try her luck and watch
as chestnuts crackle, spit
and spat in the grate,
who peels an apple to know a
lover, a husband; who before bed,
as pins are transferred from
cushion to sleeve, to aid her
sleep, her dream of him,
will pray.

*The Remains of Trentham Hall at
Trentham Gardens*

The Little Month

The 'little month' of kale,
sol monath and ritual
cleansing arrived.
The blessing of candles
was done.
Snowdrops were seen
sheltered from the fill dyke
force of snow or rain,
of white or black.
And februa, a festival forgotten,
gave way to a saint
of hearts and flowers
who used the borrowed days
of January for his feast.
And signed his note,*
  'from your Valentine'

*While in prison awaiting execution for his
 Christian beliefs, Valentine fell in love with his
warder's daughter.
 On the morning he was to be put to death,
 he gave her a note and signed it 'from your
Valentine', this is where our tradition of sending
cards on the 14th February begins.

The Lenten Days

The Lenten days arrive,
come in, Hredmonath
and let us feast with you,
goddess of winter.
Rugged, stormy month
of digging, raking and ploughing.
Mars has no quarrel, knowing
the ides that split the month
are his on which to feast.
And as lent lilies bloom
and the lamb bleats to leave,
taking* April's borrowed days,
we'll hear no more of
spite and slaughtered cows,
but delight at the
madness of the hare
as he boxes and dances
through his landscape.

*March borrowed three days from April. Folklore says that an old woman angered Mars and so the god borrowed the days to enable him to kill her cow as he hadn't succeeded during the month's original twenty-eight days.

April

Eastre monath.
The feasting month.
Bringing with it the opening of bud
on tree and flower.
It is Ostara's* month,
and the hare, her sacred creature
dances. But come first the fool,
and then the cuckoo
with his song. The swallow,**
not yet woken from his muddy rest,
is silent.
St Mark's*** eve has yet to evoke
the ghosts of those to die,
while at home in the fireglow,
a maiden may see a lover,
if fate is kind.
And George our English saint,
our hero from Palestine,
will save us from all dragons?

*Ostara, goddess of April, feast day 21st April.

** It was believed by the ancients that birds slept
in the mud of rivers throughout the winter and that
is why they were not seen.
*** St Mark's eve, April 24th.

Tri Milchi Monath

With bonfires lit, we watch winter
die in flames
as summer is received.
And in the early morning dew
a maiden will wash her face
and hope to be a queen.
Jack in the green will strut,
if there are chimney sweeps
to dress.
And in the church, a green man
may smile down.
Hobby Horses will dance
and at the Maypole,
innocence entwine.
Men, faces blackened or not,
will make steps in time.
And the hawthorn, our talisman,
shall bring forth May.

Tri Milchi Monath (Anglo-Saxon) In May when the grass was fresh and lush, cattle could be milked three times a day.

The Dry Month

Come cut the wood, ready for Solstice.
Light the bonfires, watch the leaping flame
strengthen our sun at its height.
This is our longest day.
The standing still of the sun.
Litha monath,
when the sea is calm and the breezes gentle,
when Midsummer Eve beckons.
A time of ritual and feasting,
when scattered rose petals conjure
up a lover with the dawn,
when any rose picked at sunrise
will have six months of perfect life.
This is June. Sera monath.

July

Hey monath, maed monath,
mow and make hay, gather and
dry the meadow flowers,
and on the fifteenth pray
for fine weather.
It's a day St. Swithin
has for his own, before
the swans are upped and
St. Christopher comes
to carry us safely
on life's travels.

St. Swithin's day, 15th July.
Swan upping, third weekend in July.
St. Christopher's day, 25th July.

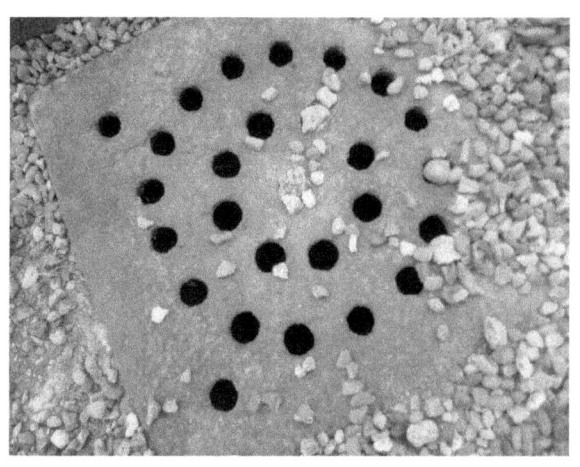

Woed Monath

The bread baked and
blessed heralds Lamass
and eleven days of feast
and fair.
A partner taken will
not bind you in marriage,
not at this date of ripening,
sultry heat and thunder.
Eleven days of cooling,
of wait and see, and
at fairs end, give thanks
for grass and grain. Mow
the fields and fill
the garner.

.

Lamass was celebrated on the 1st August. Bread was baked and blessed. Lamass is from 'Loaf Mass'. At this time you were allowed to take a partner for the days of the fair, to see if you were compatible. You did not have to marry; you could change your mind if you wished.
It was the month when grass grew apace, the month of harvest. Woed, means weed, but is taken generally to mean grass and vetch.

Macclesfield canal

Barley Month

Gerst monath–
make the brew
and drink the beer.
September–
ancient seventh
given by Rome
to Vulcan's care.
Reap the Haefest,
fill the store–
for come Michaelmas
we must ring
the curfew bell,
tell all that winter beckons.

Wyn Monath

Come gather and make wine,
October is here. The golden month
of twenty-nine fine days, of mop fairs and
dog whipping, of golden-leaf mornings
and fair afternoons.

And at its midpoint, St Luke
may watch over those who wish
to see a husband, and grant the same.

Then later, when the month
is at its end, and the falcon
has hunted, then we will
think of absent friends, of
witching hours and wait for
the saints to come.

Old Ninth

Blod monath arrived
shrouded in mist and
winter chill.
Soon the firewood
would be stacked
and the cattle
slaughtered.
And when All Saints
and All Souls had passed,
Mischief Night gone
and even before
Guy Fawkes
could be remembered,
then the beef of Martinmas
would be eaten.
Our preparation for winter
all but done.

November was originally the ninth month of the year, and was Blod Monath in Anglo-Saxon, the month when the cattle was slaughtered.

Lymm, Cheshire

Yule Monath

When St. Nicholas visits
and a Yule log
is burned to last
through thirty-one days,
when kisses are stolen
and berries taken,
when a lot is drawn
so Lord Misrule
can cause havoc,
when Saturnalia
is remembered
and trees decorated,
then will the Christ child
be born,
then will we feast
for twelve days,
then will this become
Heligh monath.

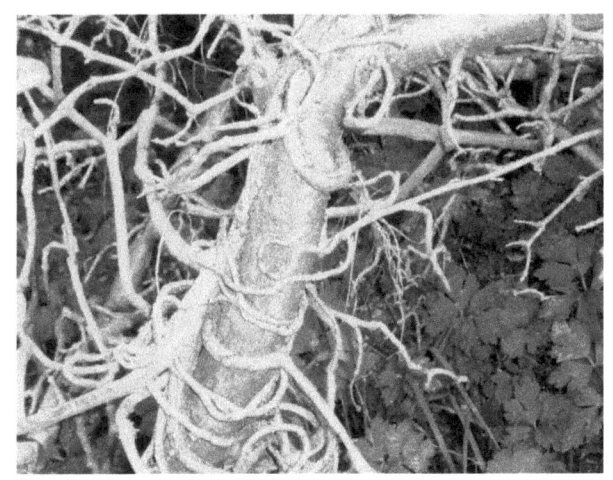

Peak Forest Canal, Marple

As a Child...

I saw...
January open her eyes on the year,
Perfect and bright.
Watched as geese skeined across
A February sky.
Marvelled at the antics
Of hares as they boxed and danced
Across a spring meadow.
Picked milkmaids, daisies and
Buttercups for a mother's bouquet.
Caught the '*sugars*' of
Willowherb and wished.
Told the time with a '*dandelion clock*',
Not knowing how fast the time
Was running on.
Smelt the woodsmoke of
Autumn, and watched it colour the days
And ease winter silently into place.
No decision needed.
But now...
Seasons merge, spring comes too soon,
Too wet, too cold, too hot.
And why? Weren't we present at all?
And nature's lost or failing battle is our own.
And so...
I saw in my childhood what
My children may not see,
My grandchildren may not know,
And my only lasting gift may be regret.

Anas Platyrhynchos

She's the whore, the single
mother; left to bring up
the family alone, no help.
A blink of his eye and
a shake of his 'D.A' and
she was a pushover, for him
and all his mates. Her neck
and body are raw from too
much attention. No point
in hiding, there is nowhere
and in any case, he always
finds her.
Every year, it's the same.

May at Tittesworth

Sunbeams light the water
and its lapping surface
becomes a glow of a million ripples,
the hinted dartings of a thousand fish.

Well worn paths, made good with
limestone, meander through wild flower
meadows, full of annual beauty,
milk maids, dandelions, buttercups, daisies.

Further on hedgerows will give way
to larger trees, and the canopy cover
is a filigree of green,
casting shade in a mottle of patchy light.

Slacken your pace; see it for what it is,
tomorrow will catch a different view
of something that is as constant
as an artist's light and shade.

May

In the half-darkness of a late winter
as the days are clamouring toward spring,
then you see them.
The tiny pale shoots of the hawthorn.
This is our native tree, it holds the
essence of generations inside itself.
It is our talisman, our defender of good
and the enemy of evil.

Soon the buds will be visible as full
bright green leaves, and when summer
comes, it will bring with it the heady scent of may.
The blossom will open into hundreds of pink-white
flowers, tumbling out the never ending barrels
of perfume into the warm air.

Ladybird

I watch you taking the sun.
You've claimed your patch on a
redundant fence post.
Your colouring is beige,
or should I say buff?
Beige is the un-dyed
wool of sheep
and you're not *ovis*.
Sixteen black spots and quite
tiny. You have a black central
line and three lateral spots on
each elytron, (the hard covering
of your wings)
these are usually merged.
The other five dots are separate
and distinct.
Your legs are brown.
A coleopterist of course,
would have known you
immediately
for what you are.
Ladybirds to me are red
with black spots, or vice versa.
You're not, but you are
a ladybird. You are
'*Tytthaspis 16-punctata*'.

The Bumble Bee

Bombus, your name
begins with Bombus.
How appealingly
descriptive.
Not knowing what
colour your tail
will be, at this
moment doesn't matter.
Bombus is what
counts, and it is
perfect. It sums up
your bobbing
roundness, your
pleasantness of
nature. You couldn't
be spiteful if
you tried, you
don't know how.
When I see
you in flight
in early spring,
I know that summer
isn't far away.
And as the nights
lengthen and
autumn beckons
I know you will

soon be leaving.
You may even die—
perish the thought.
But for now Bombus
you're here, brightening
my days, humming about
your business.
Bombus, your name
begins with Bombus.

Lizard Point

Hiding the raw, changing rock,
the coastline heath
covers its treasure–
dark-green serpentine
veined through with red and white.

And below as breakers crash,
force change and wear against
the same,
every grain is measured,
coloured, worn to smooth.

A View of Autumn

Nights lengthen.
A softened, morning
sunlight breaks through
the blind.
Bird song comes late.

To Earth, a Love Poem

In spring he saw her in a new light.
She had a glow about her.
He held her in his hands, nurtured her
and knew her. She would give freely.

She had a glow about her
and later, while she slept
covered in ermine, he watched.
He held her in his hands, nurtured her.

And later while she slept,
when there was no more to give,
he waited. He loved her, and
in spring he saw her in a new light.

Echinoderms

You take all life from your
immense, fathomless,
median disc.
Asteroidia,
spangle-tipped in salt
to the end of your arms
red-spotted markers.
No brittle stars or
basket stars but true
Asteroidia.
And in your watery-sky
environment you flourish,
live, die, regenerate,
shine brighter than any
celestial form.

Haiku. Winter theme

Sugar drifts of snow
Icy blanket of white on
Frozen twig and bough.

Notes on poems

Exits and Entrances. (Aefter Yule) Aefter Yule is the Anglo-Saxon name for January. There is obviously a nod to Janus in the title, he looking back and forwards as the year changes, old to new.

St Hilary's day is the 13th January is reputed to be one of the coldest days of the year. St Hilary was born of pagan parents. He was made Bishop Hilary of Poitiers.

The ghosts of the past who were watching us, would have remembered colder times in years gone by when it was so cold that the wine and the ale froze.

On *St Agnes eve*, 20th January, girls tried to '*see*' who their future husband would be by practising certain rituals.

January was also known as Wolf monath in the Anglo-Saxon calendar as it was the time of the year when wolves would come into the villages looking for food as it became more scarce in the countryside.

The Little Month February is a short month, Sol monath was its Anglo-Saxon name.

The 2nd February is when Candlemass is celebrated, and the candles are blessed.

Februa was an ancient festival of cleansing.

The Lenten Day Hredmonath was the Anglo-Saxon name for March. Ides of March are on the 15th of March.

Lent lilies is another name for daffodils, seen in profusion at this time of the year.

Mars was the god of war.

April Eastre monath was the Anglo-Saxon name for April.

April Fool's day is celebrated on the 1st April.

St Mark's eve is celebrated on the 24th April.

Tri Milchi Monath Tri Milchi Monath was the Anglo-Saxon name for May. It was thought that cows could be milked up to three times a day at this time of the year as the grass was green and lush.

On May Day bonfires would be lit to mark the end of winter. The dew on May Day morning was believed to have magical properties, and if you washed in it, it would keep you beautiful. The festival of the May Queen was celebrated on this day. The Jack in the Green was a man dressed head to toe in greenery, and was popular at May Day festivals, as were chimney sweeps, who would dance through the streets, their faces blackened. Hobby Horses were also seen at the May Day festivals, complete with rider. The Maypole has long been associated with May Day and was a fertility symbol. The dances around the Maypole were generally performed by children who held on to different coloured garlands that were attached to the top of the pole. As the children danced the garlands would be bound in intricate patterns.

These dances are well worth seeing, they are performed in parts of Derbyshire and some take place on Oak Apple Day in Castleton, Derbyshire. A place you should visit if you're interested in English folklore. Oak Apple Day is on the 29th May.

The Hawthorn or May is the native tree of the British Isles and is believed to have protective properties. Keep a few leaves in your pocket to ward off the evil eye.

The Dry Month Sera monath is the Anglo-Saxon name for June. The summer solstice falls usually between the 21st-24th June. Midsummer day is the 24th June. It is the longest day of the year. Midsummer Eve is on the 23rd June.

July The Anglo-Saxon name for July is Hey monath, or Maed monath. Swan-upping takes place during the third weekend in July. It is the time when the swans on the River Thames are counted.

Woed Monath Woed monath is the Anglo-Saxon name for August.

Lamass is celebrated on the 1st August. It is 'Loaf mass'. The bread was baked and blessed on this day.

Barley Month The Anglo-Saxon name for September was Gerst monath. It was the brewing month, for making and drinking beer. It was originally the seventh month of the year.

Another name from Anglo-Saxon, Haefest, means harvest.

Michaelmas is celebrated on the 29th September. A bell was rung on Michaelmas to let people know that winter was on its way.

Wyn Monath Wyn monath was the Anglo-Saxon name for October. It is the month for making wine.

St Luke's day is celebrated on the 18th October. Halloween is celebrated on the 31st October. All Saints Day is celebrated on the 1st November. All Souls day is celebrated on the 2nd November.

Old Ninth Blod monath was the Anglo-Saxon name for November. It was originally the ninth month of the year. It was the month when cattle were slaughtered. Mischief Night is celebrated on the 4th November. Martinmas is celebrated on the 11th November. Guy Fawkes or Bonfire night is celebrated on the 5th November.

Yule Monath Yule monath is the Anglo-Saxon name for December.

St Nicholas is celebrated on the 6th December. Mistletoe is a scavenger, growing on the boughs of other trees, particularly apple. It is popular as a Christmas decoration and it is traditional to kiss beneath the mistletoe at this time of year.

With each kiss a berry from the mistletoe bough is removed.

Lord Misrule is celebrated on the 17th December. Saturnalia is a festival named after the god Saturn. The feasting takes place between the 17th and the 23rd December. December is also known as Heligh monath in Anglo-Saxon, or 'Holy Month'. The twelve days of Christmas are the days we now celebrate the festivities of the Christmas period. Beginning with Christmas day, (25th December) and finishing twelve days later on the 6th January. This is the feast of Epiphany when we remember the coming of the wise men to visit and bring gifts to the infant Jesus.

Reference source used:
A Dictionary Of Saints Days, Fasts, Feasts And Festivals. By Colin Waters.
The Anglo-Saxon Year. By Arlea Hunt-Anshutz.

Other books by Margaret Holbrook

Watching and Other Stories, *Short stories, fiction*
Cul De Sac Tales, *Humour, fiction*

Website:
www.margaretholbrookwrites.weebly.com

Acknowledgments

Acknowledgments are due to the editors of the following publications in which some of these poems first appeared: *The Dawntreader, Cloudbursts.*

Milton Keynes UK
Ingram Content Group UK Ltd.
UKHW021827280823
427632UK00011B/1431